Raising Eden

Volume II

Wisdom of the Singular Truth

by

Daniel Dunn

For Further Reading

And study by this author,

Please purchase

RAISING EDEN,

Wisdom of the Eternal (Volume I)

Available from Amazon in Paperback!!

Dedication

This Book is dedicated to all of the beings and humans who have given so much behind the scenes and who will never be recognized nor known by the vast majority of people's within this world for all of their work and everything that they have given. Through their ultimate sacrifice in many cases giving their entire lives including life itself. Freedoms have been preserved and we are still here alive as a race. Because of these known and unspoken of heroes of humanity and the human race, we can continue onwards in life and we still have more time to create and maintain freedom for all because of and through their efforts. The gift they provided was time itself, our most precious resource. Now it is down to us to carry the flame and bring true freedom to this world, a world desperately in need of your light. Terra Nova (Earth) is waiting for you to dissolve the darkness with in yourself and the darkness within the world from beyond it. So our destiny can be fulfilled and EDEN can once again be rais ed into manifestation once more. Honour to the ancestor's and children yet to come!!

INTRODUCTION

This Book is VOLUME II of the RAISING EDEN wisdom series. Please read Raising Eden Wisdom of the Eternal (Book one and Volume I) if you have not done already done so, as these quotes expand upon things and they are complimentary.

These quotes of wisdom are original and were written over a long period in heightened states of stillness, in an environment of nature. The Sacred quotes from The Singular Truth within are placed upon each page one at a time as there is such power in each one. A person can use them to transform their human condition and state of being-ness to whole new higher levels for ever and because much of the pure direct communication is within the stillness and space used, not just within what is said. Thus engage it only with your heart and as less mind as possible to gain its full benefit.

Read the quotes as many times in the day as you feel necessary or memorise its very essence and replay it hour by hour. Focus on nothing but the quote throughout that day, the quote you're on or that which you have chosen randomly with feeling, to gain full advantage of its wisdom.

Through you and this initial intent, it will gain energy and live inside you like a growing seed and once activated it will become a part of your consciousness for all time. Forever from that moment forwards it will strengthen you and your BEING, altering your thoughts and life for ever more for all time, if applied daily moment to moment.

Each quote is like an onion with many profound layers. So Stay PRESENT WITH ONE QUOTE for at least the whole day to gain its full advantage, let it imbue its living energy into your being and become a part of you.

These Raising Eden Volumes were written for one purpose alone, so as to bring the human condition up to higher levels, ultimately making the world a better place for all and in a better state than when the author first birthed forth into the world. It is his lifelong mission and is still on going.

IS this not the case for us all?

For what is a Human Being if they do not try to make the world they are within a better place for one another and all life?

Give yourself to that which is necessary, that which is meaningful and vital, fulfil your destiny, carry these gems of wisdom in the very core of who you are, within your heart and soul, for the world, into the world. Apply them by example in life and spread the Wisdom quotes of the Divine Singular Truth Within, far and wide!

For the human family, all life and all that is good within the Multiverse.

Then together may we all RAISE EDEN as a Unified Human Race once again. When those who love peace can organize as good as or better than those who love war, then there shall be Peace! The future is in Your Hands! It always was!

BE L(((((O)))))VE

"One of the ultimate questions one can ask is. How PRESENT are you to your own life? How PRESENT are you to your Self? For everything comes down to this, this is ultimately what separates all of humanity"

"If you are free on the inside, you will then be able to create freedom on the outside"

"The knowledge and wisdom will be received by those who have the need for it and also the capacity"

"Every time you make a decision in life. Always ask yourself, will this improve my life?"

"Return to your original nature, return to the place where freedom and love become YOUR WORLD"

"Everything is within a different state of being. To ascend, refine your being, refine your states of being. The more refined your consciousness, the more your new state of being can permeate deeper understanding"

"As above so below, so below as above"

"Evolution = More choices of how to survive. Higher emotions give us more choices, lower emotions constrict us"

"Your job is to find and discover all of the barriers where love is unable to be expressed fully and dissolve them so it can flow"

"BE LOVE. For love is both the starting place and the end result"

"I love my love, my love inside"

"Things that serve others may not serve you and things that served you in the past may no longer serve you any longer.

So Let go of all the things that no longer serve you and replace them with things that do"

"Allow your work to serve you; do not serve your work"

"Thoughts are alive; thoughts hold the tremendous power of the whole within themselves, the power of infinity. God created the universe and all things from a single thought. Imagine what you can do?"

"Gods first task is to unburden you,

It is known as the unburdening"

"In order to experience the new,

One must make a space from the old"

"Use the wisdom within Raising Eden to transform your life positively, constructively and practically every day. For it was meant for you and now you have received it"

"Different people draw out of you different things; this is the power of

PRESENCE and STILLNESS in action"

"The mind only sees what it is prepared to see and what the body at the time has capacity for"

"When following the Singular Truth
within we are at the right place,

Doing the right thing,

At the right time"

"The human race as a whole is stuck in adolescence, it must express its creativity and especially it's LOVE, on a whole new higher level to evolve and mature"

"Peoples primary relationship needs to be with God the Creator and their primary allegiance to The Singular Truth within the individual"

"Do not spend your time and energy on conceptualizing or labelling things for it is not needed and is unnecessary. Spend your inner resources and outer resources to actualize them instead. With the full fury, fire and focus of The Singular Truth"

"A person has four pillars in life like the four legs of a table; people are only as strong as their weakest pillar. The Four pillars are Spirituality, Relationships, Health, Work/Sustainability. Most people only have one or two pillars in balance but you now have the opportunity to balance them all"

"For complete Spiritual well-being and to UNIFY within fully, is to tap your unlimited potential in each moment. The domains of the Mental, Emotional, Physical and Spiritual Domains must be engaged in daily and in balance to. IN ALL FOUR OF YOUR PILLARS, SPIRITUALITY, WORK, HEALTH AND RELATIONSHIP"

"The SPIRTUALITY PILLAR encompasses all levels of being and all other pillars, your core integrity, the foundation of LIFE.

The WORK PILLAR encompasses your worldly work and finances, how you can provide for family and sustain yourself within the world. It also encompasses your spiritual work and true purpose in the world and your purpose for being born, your mission.

Your HEALTH PILLAR applies again to all levels of being including the body, making it last as long as you can while within the world to complete your mission and tasks here.

Your RELATIONSHIP PILLAR encompasses all relationship, to yourself, the world, others and all things. This is a large arena for God is the total sum of all relationship.

Each day CHECK THESE FOUR PILLARS and make minor adjustments accordingly, this in of itself will put you ahead of most of the Human Race's current condition of consciousness. Keeping you fresh, vibrant and empowered"

"Energy is alive and conscious; it has its own specific unique signature. Thus what you focus on, your energetic focal point. Will magnetize that specific energy to you"

"Be mindful of all your thoughts and feelings for you can create better outcomes for ALL situations"

"What's alive within you is a vibrant living reality, a realm of pure consciousness, a dimension of FEELING, that can be drawn upon at any time to give you strength and light your way"

"Heal your perception, change your projection"

"The universe is a MIRROR for PROJECTIONS OF SELF both good and bad.

Therefore a powerful exercise and PRACTICE is to place mirrors around your home and talk to yourself in them.

The bad will then be projected back onto yourself. Because you can see yourself and observe yourself, you will not be left with any unresolved issues and you will not feel the need to project yourself or any negativity into the world and onto others, as most do today in our modern world, You can work through your own thoughts and stuff you need to deal with like this when needed.

By doing this powerful practice you will learn quickly, evolve quickly and master yourself to a very high degree.

Then the best part of yourself that is left, the good and only the good will be projected into the world as a gift for all as you become a master to a high degree of projection of self"

"PRESENCE, PROJECTION and PATIENCE are three foundational stones of any powerful spirituality. To understand these forces wholeheartedly will set you apart from most

Beings and give you a clear advantage"

"You and all beings have but Two choices in Life. To be PRESENT to yourself, others and to the reality in which you live or to not be"

"The Level of PRESENCE within your being and each moment is all that separates the full spectrum of humanity and all life.

How PRESENT are you to yourself?

How PRESENT are you to others?

How PRESENT are you to the Universe and to the reality in which you find yourself?"

"How PRESENT are you to yourself? For PRESENCE and RESPONSIBILITY go hand in hand"

"The further you are from INTERNAL STILLNESS, the further you are from God and your True Self"

"Relationships require work daily and PRESENCE. Do not allow them to go stagnant; always be PRESENT to yourself and others fully, all of the time"

"During your life here,

What did you do for yourself?

What did you do for others?

What did you do for the world?

What did you do for All Life?

Correct this if you have overlooked anything"

"While engaging in love we bring more of it into the world. By engaging in compassion, kindness, and caring for all life and living things we are bringing more of these things into the world. Bring forth these things and do not hold back, it will wash over the world and everything within it, changing it and healing it for all time, it is that simple"

"The universe is full of magical things, which are waiting for us to evolve, grow up more and discover/explore them"

"Mentors are important in life; they speed up the evolutionary process, offering a quantum leap in the evolution of being"

"Mentorship is a very important thing in life as it helps amplify and enhance the journey to Self and the Singular Truth within, on the path of life. It provides a faster transfer of knowledge from one being to another for the continuation of the species, thus more powerful deeper and meaningful wisdom is gained for all, later in life"

"It's the action of doing that thrust's us forth into more action"

"Once it flows,

IT FLOWS!

This is the Consciousness Cascading effect"

"The human body naturally heals itself from all ills. It does not need anything adding to it or taken away from it to be perfect and for it to have this God gifted ability. All human mind is a distortion of its prime function"

"Knowing your destiny right now would destroy you. Because you do not yet have the capacity required to fulfil it and you do not yet have the skills you're going to learn at some point in the future to complete it. Not even the wisest know their destiny and the details of the journey. Because it is a matter for the heart not the mind, in order to be able to fulfil it"

"Every year, every month, every week, every day, every hour, for the totality of your whole life, get in true relationship with your higher self and in alignment with The Singular Truth within"

"All experiences create stability; the more experience the more stability. Each experience has a weight overall that helps stabilise all thought and emotion. Thus the more weight, the more stability, but only when taken impersonal and as a learning curve"

"Fully immerse yourself in the PRESENT, it is a gift and that is why it is called THE PRESENT"

"You must find your own therapeutic practices, for comfort, stability, happiness and fulfilment"

"Give them no energy; they cannot sustain the system without your participation. Always be conscious where your energy is flowing"

"The journey of life is infinite growth and expansion every day and thereon after"

"Everything is Consciousness and

is in a state of Being"

"Race is a manmade control mechanism, for those who desired power and control over humanity. There is but ONE RACE, the human race. This unity is how God the creator sees things"

"Do not focus nor fight those who do no harm nor ever have. Focus your energy against those who are doing harm right now, by not participating in what they say or do and pouring energy into what you're doing, your own creation"

"Learn to say NO.

Give no time or any energy away to anything that destroys your spiritual integrity and is doomed to fail. Do not participate!"

"To be free to love and create is what all people require. We are born in the image of God the Master Creator, which is pure love. We were designed to gather experience and to create"

"The part of you abiding with and that never left God the Creator, that is contained within the deeper heart, has all the answers"

"Open your heart and soul to the domain of your inner knowing. The domain that links to the domain of all that can be known"

"Come as a return of the visionary, a return of sacred legend, a return of the divine myth"

"Connect to the powerful source of your CREATIONAL HEART.

Forge new ways of creating, seeing and being.

POWERFUL BEINGS create everything"

"Master to a high degree the arts of the unseen, in the realms of the seen"

"No lies, no deceit, no agenda, no untruths. Just be and live truth. Truth, truth, TRUTH"

"Darkness's shadow evil. Is but a corruption of The Singular Truth within, therefore there is always an opposite light born to oppose it"

"Evil will always present itself as good or it would not be accepted by people"

"The Shetu are the predator consciousness of the Great Abyss. Their gold is energy and they plunder consciousness"

"The Shetu infiltrate into worlds and beings like a disease; they fuse themselves into the fabric of reality and consciousness itself. They are the disharmony to Gods harmony"

"Everything is consciousness on different levels and contains differing levels of awareness to hold its state of being. Every Being, every Planet, every Star, every Galaxy, every Universe. Every Object"

"Nurture over nature is a good philosophy. In its practice and through its example, it shows when you give to something greater than yourself, anything is possible"

"Learn to channel and direct your energy properly onto meaningful pursuits and endeavours, do not allow the ego to channel and direct your consciousness onto wasted pursuits and endeavours"

"You only have a certain amount of time and energy within life. Do not waste it"

"Build a REAL WORLD,

A REAL LIFE.

With truth,

The Singular Truth within,

as its foundational stone"

"The heart must rule the mind, for the mind must be restrained by the knowledge, wisdom and patience of the heart. Without love, without heart, power will always corrupt and destroy"

"Colonisation is not just a physical thing that only happens within the world, they also try to colonise your mind, body and soul"

"Colonize every part of your

own body, mind & being

with love.

BRING FORTH REALITY ITSELF"

"Sharing everything you know is your duty, your DNA contains a living library. The ancients understood this well, it was their culture and tradition"

"As long as money is allowed to be printed out of thin air and people are apathetic to the truth, The LIVING SINGULAR TRUTH within themselves. A few evil men/beings have full control over your life, your children and your future"

"All the systems that subdue a person enslave the spirit and try to control all aspects of your being, upon all levels. Plus those who architected it, it's creators, need you. We do not need them"

"Step into your own powers, God the Creator gave you power with a purpose. Occupy every part of yourself, on all levels, forever. Indefinitely.

Never give up ground again. People and the world need you"

"When you walk within your own God given power and shine fully as an example, it allows the hearts of others to awaken to their own light. It gives them permission on a subconscious level and thus they can engage in their own journey to the True Self and The Singular Truth within"

"Antarctica was once a beautiful chain of lush green tropical islands; it was the seat of a wondrous and highly advanced civilization of the ancients. This civilization was worldly and galactic in nature. It built cities based upon the perfect geometric model, the circle, as it is the most efficient shape for energy to flow. These ruined cities were once utilized by the indigenous and aboriginal populations. Not only can the ruins for this circle design be found all over the world, but upon all moons and planets in this solar system"

"Anchor yourself deeply into The Singular Truth within. Stand within your own power and domain fully, we are so powerful. The power of our thoughts and emotion creates reality. Be forever cautious and vigilant however, for there are dark forces that hide within the creation itself"

"Sometimes the effect is felt before the cause. By taking action now, you can create alternative realities and timelines. Beings sometimes emerge in our world from these realities to help create freedom within this timeline, so we can create where they have just come from"

"Time is not linear,

It's a river that flows

BOTH WAYS"

"Where water flows, food grows"

"Something is only ever worth as much as somebody is willing to pay for it"

"A heavenly abode of inner mystery,

Universal knowledge and timeless

Wisdom of the eternal,

Exists inside each and every one of us.

Bring it forth!"

"Own your sorrows and pain, your stumbles and your falls, your defeats and your losses. They are yours and belong to you"

"Science will never know all the answers. Because science is Ego/Mind based. Knowledge of the heart domain is not accessible by the mind. God the Creator made the creation this way purposely so it is always beyond any form of control and outside the reach or measure by man or any being trying to corrupt it fully"

"Let everything unfold naturally and the power, potency and effects of all manifestations is far greater"

"Mankind will continue becoming weakened, diseased and disempowered, the species will perish if it continues to walk in the shadow of its own enlightenment. The tides are turning against us, who will you turn to for strength, power and stability? The Singular Truth within, that part of you that never left God"

"In a Culture of Life it creates peace, harmony, stability, certainty, pure bliss, through stillness. It cultivates and creates a powerful Self Identity based upon truth itself, an identity and centre that is the most powerful force in the universe and that can never be broken.

The Culture of Death however, such as within this world currently, sucks all your energy, needs your participation and offers nothing valuable in return. It has no source for life, creates a false identity based upon falsehood. It takes by force, creates chaos because it pays for it to do so to survive, it has no real centre or power.

Create a Culture of Life, pour all your energy daily and participate no more in the Culture of Death, thus it will collapse the Culture of Death altogether"

"Constantly reinvent yourself and your work or become extinct. Let your creativity flow and be free. Life is constantly moving/breathing. A stagnant life destroys creativity, it destroys love,

it destroys everything"

"Do not force creation; allow your creations to emerge naturally and in their own time"

"Do not desolate your soul by participating and getting lost in the worlds Culture of Death. Join and create the Culture of Life. Then abundance can emerge for all and upon all levels, for you shine that from within"

"Never base your decisions on fear, but always on love. For fear contracts manifestations and if you follow that path it will always lead you into a worse situation and reality than the one you find yourself within right now. THAT is how manifesting reality works!"

"How the world currently is today and the state it exists within, is a direct reflection and accumulation of the decisions based either upon Fear or Love of every single human being and all the creatures, since the beginning of time"

"There never was such a thing as survival of the fittest. It was always survival of The MOST ADAPTABLE"

"And the lands of the elementals, the inner worlds and outer worlds were all but lost"

"I'm looking for wisdom; I'm open to them special moments of inspiration in the day, when it comes through from a higher power, day by day. The simple but direct teachings that are like gems for all of us, I allow anything that can be used to uplift humanity to come through and I record it. We are but the channel for God the Creator, your Greater Deeper Mind, Higher Self and The Singular Truth within are the source"

"It's very important to be open to receive. If you are open to receive then there is a space inside for treasures of the cosmos and even miracles themselves can come true and manifest"

"Police, military personal, and politicians are people in fancy dress who enforce the will of the architects of the system. Through their actions, they are ones who support the System of Death and who have abandoned the Culture of Life."

"There is no middle man between you and the Creator, all men are created equal. Do not allow other people or beings to tell you how it is or to get in between you and what you know is good, wise, right and true."

"Focus is very important, it draw's onto thee the full potential of all your creative ability, allowing the greatness of The Singular Truth within, your Higher Self and Greater Deeper Mind to flow and thus be manifest into the world"

"Do not reinforce and help build the reality of others if they have no spiritual integrity and it's based upon lies. Give them no time, no energy and no attention; do not participate at all on any level.

Build your own reality, live your own reality, plant the Seeds of Truth, while staying true to the Singular Truth within. Then the truth will grow and sprout forth as an unstoppable, unshakeable, unmovable force. A power of truth that has the ability to build a whole new world based on truth and love for all"

"Do not concern yourself with those who only serve themselves and get rich at the expense of others and their own soul. Only concern yourself with your creations for the greater good of all, that serve humanity as a whole"

"In this world people overload themselves with too much information. They become over saturated and when their capacity is full, they shut down and cannot function.

BE MINDFUL!"

"Build your capacity for Truth and different things through the process of Being and doing, every single day.

Practice, practice, practice, PRACTICE!"

"We are far more powerful than any of this darkness and evil, it is THAT very reason WHY it is all done to us in the first place. Our Power is Unlimited"

"Slowly with unshakeable patience, day by day, refine yourself and your being from one state of awareness into another. Establishing a relationship with your Higher Self, you're Greater Deeper Mind, Your True Self. All spiritual growth and unification of Self is a marathon not a sprint"

"Wash and bathe in the peaceful, relaxing, tranquil waters of stillness. For it is the PURE energy of God the Creator itself"

"Through All the pain, All the suffering, All the losses, All the Trials, All the betrayals, All the tragedy. Keep going, never stop.

Forge your destiny and shake the pillars of the Wisdom Halls of Eternity. This is your moment, you made it"

"Always be expansive in everything you do, think, feel or say. Do not destroy possibilities or limit yourself ever, this in of itself will birth an expanded Greater Life"

"Never shrink and dim your own Divine Sacred Light, so others feel more comfortable. Shine your light fully, always and all of the time, it is a world in need of it"

"One of the saddest most heart breaking things to see and feel for the cosmos, earth and humanity. One of its biggest unseen and unspoken sorrows is when a person either loses their God gifted life prematurely or sleep walks through their life and the unlimited untapped potential of an individual. The vibrant living ocean of infinite possibility becomes lost. Their gifts undelivered"

"Follow God the Creators example in all things, God the Creator is in no rush, it does not have to be anywhere fast. So when it comes to engaging with others within the world, allow things to unfold naturally, unforced and in a benevolent way.

God the Creator is perfect and that part of God, the perfection that is of God is within you too. THAT is the Singular Truth within, the torch in the heart of man, to teach, counsel, comfort and guide. It's a Greater Deeper Mind, Your Higher True Self"

"It is the part of you that never left God the Creator that you now must reclaim and bring forth back into the world. The Singular Truth within"

"We are surrounded and immersed with many different worlds, both inner and outer worlds, all occupying the same space at the same time, simultaneously. Each vibrating upon its own unique harmonic vibration"

"Human beings make too much noise, if they are to create freedom and survive in this hostile universe, they must learn to be more discreet. They must be self-sufficient and more responsible on a day-to-day basis for every decision made and action taken"

"Heroes step forwards into the light, during times of the greatest darkness. Reminding us and shining as examples of the greatness we can be a part of, once we decide to unshackle ourselves and unbind our True Heart"

"Everything in existence, all of consciousness including human beings themselves are either becoming a cube or a circle.

Becoming whole and free or enslaved and fragmented"

"Intention is the brother of attention"

"Intent is very important, intent is a LIVING FORCE. When something is IMBUED WITH INTENT it is imbued with life, it is this PRESENCE that causes evolution and transforms all things. Imbue your creations with intent of the Highest Order"

"Attention in the NOW has great POWER beyond conception. PRESENCE in the moment makes the impossible possible, the improbable probable, the unworkable workable. It makes everything POSSIBLE"

"Every being has its own unique energy signature and frequency it vibrates at. All stars do, all planets do. Everything is alive and is singing its own melody"

"Everything is within God The Creator, there is nothing outside of God. Everything in the multiverse is in a transformational state changing from one state to another"

"Never bind your soul to the finite and temporal by doing actions and behaviour that will do so. SPIRITUAL INTEGRITY is what you must preserve at all costs"

"You can be a follower and a leader all at once. Be a follower of The Singular Truth within, your Greater Deeper Mind and Higher Self. Then be a leader when you have learned some of the wisdom and lessons it provides, to apply it within the world. Never follow other people or give power away to external influence on any level, because even the greatest of beings are guides only, leading you into your own empowerment. All responsibility starts and ends with you"

"Do not take serious nor follow the rules, from beings whose lives are built on lies, who take wrongful action, who do not live in balance with themselves, others or the world. Who are unwise and who do not put their spirituality at the centre of their lives. What you have inside you is far greater and more powerful than what they can imagine or begin to comprehend. Do not let them try to keep you down, or hold you back. You are far more powerful and greater than what they could ever be"

"If you feel you do not fit into this world or are destined for great things, BOTH ARE TRUE. You contain within you seeds of greatness, you are here to birth a whole new reality, you are here to Raise Eden within this world"

"If you understand the truths of things more than those around you, they will think you're crazy when you speak of things they have low awareness on or have overlooked themselves. Those not on a spiritual path of expansion of being, do not comprehend the truth because they are already shut down and not open to it. Only deal and work with those who are open to receive"

"Even something as simple as a book, has the ability to alter the course of history if its knowledge is applied wholeheartedly by those who read it"

"Master Your CREATIVE FOCUS.

As long as you are creating and loving,

Destiny belongs to thee"

"Focus upon your better angels, do not be pulled down into the dark depths of oblivion. But if oblivion should meet thee,

Engage it with love"

"The states and emotion of man are like weather and changing seasons within this world. We all have springs, summers, autumns and winters. Identify the songs of your life and direct yourself accordingly"

"You cannot live and edit your life to be within a one seasoned world. All seasons are created with great purpose to enrich, strengthen, test you, refine you,
To expand your consciousness and thus evolve you into the potential of what you already truly are"

"Everybody is a messenger and carry's a deeper communication, a deeper teaching to give"

"Seek the extraordinary,

Live the extra ordinary"

"Allow the universe to flow the vibrant living water of Eternal Higher Consciousness through your being. Create an opening, create a space. When you create a space inside for your Deeper Greater Mind to emerge and get into relationship with your Higher Self. Higher Consciousness will flow"

"Cultivate an environment, an environment of growth so all your skills, natural abilities, positive attributes and divine untapped destiny are brought forth as a gift for all within the world and cosmos"

"Those living from the shallow surface ego finite human mind and those living from their Deeper Greater Mind, the Infinite Heart, The Singular Truth within, and that are in true relationship flowing their Higher Self into the world, are as different form one another as night is from day. Never make the mistake thinking they are like one another at all"

"FOCUS is POWER, you must direct it and not allow it to direct you. To be able to direct the power of your thoughts and emotion anytime, anywhere.

IS EVERYTHING"

"In the War on Consciousness itself,

Take action, action, action.

Every day, always!

Without question"

"The beast system of Babylon cannot survive without you; you are used as a source of energy to sustain it. It is an evil dark parasitic predator vampire. Do not participate in anything that is bad for your Higher Consciousness and True Self. FOCUS upon your creation, with the FULL TOTALITY of your energy"

"Birthing something into the world is always messy. It is a very hard thing to build a whole new reality, but worth it. One must have a pure vision, hold it with unshakeable focus and patience against all the odds, and like a seed nourish, sustain and protect it. If you can allow the vision to germinate in its own time, allow its seeds to fly in the winds of divine mystery and time unafraid, then others will join you in its creation. When two or more people are involved in a dream, it is no longer a dream but a reality"

"You are a creator being, gifted with the infinite powers of the Creation itself. You can imagine and achieve anything at any time you do so conceive of, your power is immense"

"Do not create a space or environment that allows any negative energy to flourish, hate or anger etc. Create environments, for love, compassion, peace, truth and all positivity and positive attributes to flourish"

"For true wisdom and knowledge of the Eternal, look for the natural things that never change within this ocean of change"

"Nature is a reflection of the human energy field upon the outside; in nature you will find plants and mixes of plants to heal all disease and ills. Because life is music everything is vibrating, and all one must do is just find the right note or tones to heal all things"

"If you dream, always dream big. If you ever want to do something, do it in an EPIC way"

"Paranoia is a higher form of perception and awareness. As long as it does not direct your actions, it is a good thing to have"

"Love always comes first and then power, in that order. Then you do not abuse what you have and are a force for good in the world and universe. For it is restrained by something Greater than that of itself"

"We are the beginning and the end,

The today and the tomorrow"

"One is Two and Two is Three,

All is One and One is all,

Flying Upon the Golden path of Eternity"

"We are not perfect, but contain perfection within. Human existence is not about being perfect but about making mistakes, learning, experiencing and expanding our awareness on this level. It's about being refined back to the Divine Sacred Perfection that is already there"

"All new technology invented or recovered from the ancient world, or other intelligent races, is always checked for its military applications before it is commercialised, if it sees the light of day at all. Some of the technology has been proven and is extensively documented to be at least 50 to 100 Years ahead of what is available in the public domain"

"Even negative emotions can be used for great good and positively if you direct them and do not allow them to direct you"

"The greater the effects on humanity and the cosmos that your creativity will have, the more tired you will feel at the outset of the birthing process in direct and in proportion to its effects in the future, ahead of time"

"Perceived separation from God the Creator, one another and reality itself, is the Prime root of all suffering"

"God the Creator see's all things from within side, not outside"

"Every small act of random kindness (ARK), helps everyone and heals everyone through time"

"Focus all your energy on your own creation, do not fight nor resist those who have made you their enemy. Simply stand always fully in your own power, their creations can't or won't last. But yours will"

"Give yourself to something greater than yourself, in this environment you will always then be growing and expanding significantly in all aspects of your being"

"There is never NOTHING going on,

There is always SOMETHING happening.

Simply, LISTEN."

"There is no scale on which to measure where a person is on their journey to True Self. So do not try. Beings have just got to do what they have to do, it is naturally inbuilt and not even the most wise can see the whole picture.

So do not judge, because there is always a whole lot more going on than what one can see"

"Imagine a world where your creations are not stymied or shackled, where all are helped to achieve their full potential by one another. Where it's understood the higher one got the better for all. Live THAT now!"

"It is either a yes or a no.

Do or do not. There is no try.

There is no middle ground"

"Peace through awareness of

God the Creator and the Creation"

"There is no such thing as death.

Energy is but the movement of consciousness, it cannot be destroyed.

Do you really think consciousness can be?"

"If you never apply the knowledge you learn, then its wasted energy and knowledge.

A waste of our gifts and of our purpose in the world that was meant for both"

"Keep as much ego based mind out of the equation as possible, for all ego based mind is a replacement for the Greater Deeper Mind and Singular Truth within, that which you are reclaiming"

"Do not allow the world to pull you into its Darkness, Chaos or Evils. Pull the world into your Creation, Love and Peace"

"This is Dream Time,

Dream EDEN"

"People are real"

"It is uphill every stage of the way into the divine mystery of your true self.

Expand, learn, expand, learn."

"Truth is a way of Life, a way of being. People will have to change how they live and do things if they are to go higher to the very heart of their True Self"

"In life there is no rehearsal,

BE PRESENT to yourself,

Always"

"Eat healthy LIVING FOOD. Never dead food. The more LIVING the food, the more PRESENCE. Thus the healthier it is for you"

"From field to plate within five minutes. The faster you can eat food from the ground the more energy, LIFE FORCE and PRESENCE within it. As the energy has less time to dissipate"

"Only a fool reacts, a wise person responds"

"Understand.

Overstand.

Innerstand"

"Freedom is a LIVING PROCESS one must be directly involved in to create and maintain it"

"Spiritual integrity is important to exert a big influence upon others and the world with minor influence on you"

"God the Creator knows us through our actions, words and deeds. Through our works and the fruits they bear. Through this journey of life and its experiences, we come to know ourselves"

"There is no such thing as failure; you only fail when you give up. But at the same time do not waste you energy on meaningless pursuits"

"The only constant in the universe is change, life is constantly moving. It requires forward momentum and velocity, life cannot stagnate.

Once life stagnates there is only one direction one goes, backwards,

Devolution"

"Give.. Give… give, as soon as you stop giving ENERGY AND PRESENCE the fractal holograph deteriorates over time. Eventually all manifestations and realities shrink over time and collapse in on themselves causing a down turn in all pillars and aspects of life"

"How you say things is important, tailor your communication to those you are speaking to"

"People can only learn from the level of capacity they have reached at the time of hearing the information and truth. They require experience in life before they can accept more truth"

"BE the original resonator"

"PRESENCE is the POWER OF STILLNESS.

Different people draw out of you different things. If you have PRESENCE it will draw out of people all the things they have yet to deal with, to the surface"

"Chaos must be, it always gets worse before it gets better. When it gets dark, do not worry or despair for it is but the breaking of the soil into the sunlight"

"The more wise and powerful the being, the more quiet one will appear to become. As their energy is precious and reserved"

"PRESENCE, THE SINGULAR TRUTH, is a living force, it is a powerful ally"

"BE PRESENT TO YOURSELF, ALWAYS"

"Hollywood is a weapon of war created by the military. The industrial military complex and Hollywood are the same war machine binded to each other and go hand in hand"

"Hollywood is a military apparatus, without keeping people entertained one cannot conquer"

"Hollywood and the music industry always release movies and music with two meanings. One for your conscious mind and the other for your subconscious"

"Society creates dependency, it sucks energy from the vulnerable and does everything it can to keep them dependant"

"Creators and Builders,
Destroyers and Predators.
That is THIS WORLD. Use discernment
with all people and beings you meet"

"There are forces in the world preventing people from creating solutions and living them every day. BE MINDFUL."

"Everybody is a star and has a singularity inside themselves that shines energy outwardly with abundance. When a polarity shift occurs, that singularity implodes unto itself like a black hole. That energy is then pulled downwardly pulling the person into fear, confusion, chaos and sometimes depression. People define this today as mental illness of which it is not"

"Centre yourself, centre your being. Direct your thoughts, emotion, feeling and action. Focus on stillness for the power of its stability and certainty. You are a living star and contain and ocean of vibrant living pure consciousness within to be tapped into at any time. Allow your True Self to flow"

"Do not spend too much time in your mind, in what we call the mental environment. Direct yourself and find balance that works for you and your level of consciousness at that time"

"To resolve a question, it requires a greater consciousness and a more expanded awareness to solve it than that of the original point when asking the question in the first place"

"Those who have anchored points of consciousness in this realm or perceived unfinished business will always be anchored here on some level, unable to move onto the next level of existence. Until their business is concluded"

"God the Creator isolates parts of its own energy to give rise to all form, dimension and being. The Creators love for you is infinite and LIFE is the most precious gift given to any being"

"Guard and protect life at all costs, it is the most precious gift"

"Energy, light and dimension are just a tool God The Creator uses to manifest thought.

Everything is consciousness, everything is made of thought. Dreams within dreams, we are the very imagination of ourselves"

"No matter how dark the storm gets, how chaotic or how destructive it seems, Abide with God the Creator"

"The human race is not civilized yet; wars, politics, religion and poverty are still rampant"

"Your consciousness is far more powerful than any directed energy weapon, beam or wave that is fired upon you or that can be fired upon you. Your Consciousness is far, far more powerful. Focus on your true self and true heart, the Singular Truth within. Thus you cannot be controlled or manipulated"

"Those who have strong attachment to the Singular Truth within their Deeper Greater Mind and are in true relationship with this Higher Self, will under pressure become like a diamond of consciousness. While those with a weak connection to the Divine Spirit in themselves will fracture and splinter in consciousness"

"ALL ARE ONE. One must give self to others or to something greater than what oneself is. Through this act of giving one is expanding more into their own potential and self, thus this outward growth and expansion leads to happiness and stability. You become more powerful upon this path of infinite expansion of self, infinitely expanding into more of what you truly already are. Everything"

"All is ONE. Altruism is the quickest path to happiness. For in this kindness and willingness to give freely, Love expands in being, the quickest it can into the power of Self and in a stable manner. But It must all be done from the heart and not a place of mind"

"Do not live in your mind.

Comparing oneself to others destroys happiness.

Live in your heart"

"Conserving resources on our world is of prime importance. If we are dependent upon resources from elsewhere in the world or other worlds in the galaxy, freedom will always be lost"

"Local commitment, global responsibility for all issues within our world"

"Bring no harm to others, to yourself or to the environment or upon any level. That is one of God the Creators prime commands"

"We are supposed to be the stewards, caretakers of the Earth and Guardians of Life. Get in alignment with this"

"Underneath the deserts of the world are vast oceans of water, the water has simply fell deep beneath the surface, that is why the surface ground is desert"

"The universe is expanding because its awareness is expanding. The human being and all life is a focal point so the universe can experience itself. Thus in this symbiotic relationship, we expand and create reality together as one. Forever growing in awareness and expanding infinitely"

"The SPIN within the two strands of DNA pulling towards SOURCE in the higher dimensions is what produces gravity and holds stars together. Thus DNA if tampered with will cause star implosion in the future. This is the Meaning of EVERYTHING IS ONE, linked macrocosmically to the microcosm"

"Like people, civilizations have a life cycle and go through different stages of life.

"Every thought is a powerful LIVING BEING and has its own life"

"Awaken the singularity with inside yourself; we are the singularity of prophecy long since spoken of"

"All thoughts are linked, they each have their place, there is no such thing as a random thought"

"Be mindful of thoughts that you perceive as random, for they are with purpose and sometimes reveal the future before it happens"

"We are all suffering on some level.

Time=suffering. Thus the purpose of you within this world and universe is to reduce suffering"

"Your life is a symphony; you can move the music, notes, tones and chords around to get different manifested results"

"If you want something knew to manifest in life simply make space for it in the symphony of life to do so"

"Energy is always shifting in relationship to oneself and all the other binded relationships experienced throughout your life. Each relationship has a chord, move around or stop the chords to get new relationships that serve you on your journey of empowerment of true self"

"The repulsion effect of magnetism is an equal and opposite reflection to the connection and attraction"

"It is called attachment because relationships bind to ones being"

"Everything is evolving; Everything has life, all energy's. When it comes to attachments of people and items, plus your possessions.

Allow them to be free. Do not allow attachments to bind to your being and drain your energy's nor your items to eventually possess you.

Let them go when your heart says to do so or the very things you own will end up owning you"

"In stillness use the binds of relationship to feel and perceive all the information about all relationships that you have. Information about the past, present and future can be known. In stillness all things can be known"

"True Relationships are not chosen by your mind, they are magnetized to you at the right time naturally by following your heart"

"Choose your relationships wisely with heart, all true relationships are about growth and growing into oneself and should be engaged within only for this purpose. Do not engage in relationships that will break, destroy you, drain you of energy and life, or weaken you"

"Light and sound are the same thing, they are both forms of light carrying a communication, we just perceive it differently with our sense"

"Everything is communication.

Everything is relationship.

Everything is energy.

Energy is consciousness.

Everything is linked and is ONE"

"Listen carefully within and you will hear echoes of the past, see reflections of the future. Calling out to you"

"Meditation is one of the most important things a human needs to do to create peace inside and within the universe. It creates full stability and inner certainty"

"Destiny is evolution attained"

"Allow your circle of love and compassion to embrace all life"

"Train to use the singular truth within, the Greater Deeper Mind, to keep you out of danger ahead of time. It is an early warning system and is the master guide for protection of one self and those you love"

"Train in stillness meditation daily, without question. This in of itself is the greatest thing one can do to increase your own power and amplify all your inherent skills and natural abilities"

"The more stillness meditation you do, the more sensitive an instrument you will become. The more sensitive, the more powerful"

"Take time out each day and upon each hour for the Singular Truth within, Your Deeper Greater Mind, and Higher Self to emerge"

"It does not matter where you are in space or time, your Inner Divine Self and the Singular Truth within can be tapped into. It is the ultimate source of power and protection accessible at anytime, anywhere with focus"

"Within the human experience are four realms that need to be mastered fully to a high degree. The physical realm in which we live. The realm of the mind, the realm of emotion and the realm of the spirit"

"Most are not aware of the realm of the mind, the Mental Environment. Yet it is through this realm where all evil arises and where people are influenced, hijacked and taken over completely"

"In the spiritual realm all thoughts and beings are equal, but in our world and universe that is strongly governed by the mental environment where most beings operate within their surface shallow ego mind. The more focused concentrated minds influence and dominate the weaker ones"

"Thoughts are powerful Living things, creatures with immense power. God created the entire universal spectrum of experience and time from one Original thought. Imagine what you can do with a single thought?"

"Whatever you focus and engage upon, you become over time.

Focus is binding"

"Focus binds energy to oneself"

"Practice patience, patience, patience"

"Let the Singular Truth and universe be your guide, listen to its will. Destiny will reveal itself as you walk it; it requires no mind, only heart"

"Destiny unfolds naturally like a flower, it requires great patience. Do not try to force it or this resistance against its true pace will explode it in your face and bring harmful manifestations unto thee"

"The closer you draw upon different energies, the more they infuse into your being and you become them. Choose wisely"

"Energy gets imbued onto objects and environments; it can be done purposely or sometimes is done by accident"

"When a traumatic event happens somewhere, the energy of the trauma gets imbued into the environment. Like a record it plays again and again over time. The highly sensitive can feel, hear and sometimes see through vision what occurred"

"Connect to the Singular Truth within; become sensitive through the power of stillness every day. Listen to the subtle fluctuations of positive and negative energies to guide your actions and your life"

"Put time, energy, and pure focus into all those abilities you wish to amplify. Strengthen them daily with unshakeable focus"

"Everything that can manifest will manifest. Fears and dreams"

"One can be light-hearted and serious at once. Without this lightness of heart your destiny would be too much for one to bear and its burden would send you insane"

"Do not fall prey to ego over the heart. It requires constant control, vigilance, and foresight to stay on the Golden Path of the Singular Truth within"

"A great weapon is to turn ones perceived enemy to your cause, to use their knowledge against them. Even the greatest warriors on the path of the Singular Truth, connected to the Deeper Greater Mind and in true relationship with their Higher Self, can fall to their ego consciousness. Always be mindful constantly, moment to moment"

"When following your destiny and you're on a path that seems familiar, a familiar path. It is because you have been on it before, you have seen it before, you have lived it before. You are not creating a new path or relationship, but are reclaiming an already established one"

"Anybody can fall and be claimed by their ego consciousness, no matter how powerful. Create powerful relationships to prevent this fall. Relationships inside yourself, relationships with others, and Relationships to places and things within the world itself"

"Balance is the master key. Never over indulge, the indulgences of a vain mind can break and destroy you. Balance all things and upon all levels in life"

"Light and dark are the same thing, there are no true labels or absolutes in life"

"The capacity for good or evil is within all creatures, belonging to any named or labelled group will not change what you are at your core"

"The Singular Truth within provides you with objectivity. Objectivity is a Key to Empowerment"

"To be objective is to be empowered, however only when one brings no harm to oneself or others. For if harm is brought upon oneself or others, there is no difference between objectivity and insanity"

"The system says to be objective to oneself show's that one is crazy. This is incorrect however, as the system itself wants you to be within ego consciousness always to control you. Only when one is objective and seeks to harm or be destruction is one crazy. For they have no compassion, remorse, or guilt for the suffering they create"

"Connect to the Singular Truth within the Greater Deeper Mind; establish a relationship with your Higher Self. Be objective and protect all life, this is your duty"

"Trauma leaves an imprint upon a person or an environment, to heal it requires at least an equal and opposite force"

"If you fulfil your destiny and follow the Golden Thread within, the consequences of the Singular Truth inside yourself will long be felt in this world and universe, long after you have left this mortal coil"

"Be as ferocious as a hurricane, with tenacity of a lion and with the subtleties of distant star light. Eternal glory awaits!"

"There will always be others to replace the minions of darkness. That is why those with a powerful Singular Truth within, utilizing their Greater Deeper Mind, and who are in true relationship with their Higher Self must step into the domain and hold the space indefinitely for all"

"Different energies are drawn to different places. If you feel a pull towards a different place or person it is because they offer growth for your soul. The place or person has something you require as you may have something they/it requires. It is your destiny"

"Be mindful of all you communicate, words spoken and tone, they have the power to heal or destroy"

"When darkness shrouds its cloak over events and comes forth, you will feel the energy pull back out of the area. This will give you advanced warning ahead of time. It is the deep breathe before the plunge"

"Be mindful and vigilant always. The deep breathe before the plunge will give you advanced warning of any ambush"

"How we handle love is a measure of who we are. Love makes you powerful"

"Abide with the Singular Truth within, always create a domain within, larger than the domain or box of control they try to put you within. This is the secret to resisting all forms of attack, for then you are always far more powerful and greater than them"

"Listen deeply to the Singular Truth within, it will give you prior warning to the energy of beings, their intentions and alignment to good or bad as they move or approach"

"Different people, places and objects draw out of you different things. Flashbacks of past, present and future will occur and be brought to the surface to be resolved at the right time"

"The Singular Truth is a familiar path; it is a natural path of healing and completion. The path of unity of self"

"The younger one starts training in the Singular Truth within, embodying the Deeper Greater Mind, and establishing a relationship with Their Higher Self, the more possibilities it allows later on in life to be able to manifest. As all possibilities are still alive and are not blocked by the ego mind. This allows even deeper insights, deeper wisdom and deeper skills, plus abilities to shine forth"

"Do not surrender to fear, negative emotions or thoughts, or they will dominate your fate. Surrender onto the positive attributes of oneself and the Singular Truth within so you are a conduit and it works through you."

"You gain the strengths of that which you surrender onto within. Be wise"

"Unite within the shadow and the light. Do not become an extreme of either. Balance in the stillness at the centre of self is the ultimate power"

"All have light within and a shadow, we are all capable of anything. The more you think you are good and deny the shadow the more the shadow will grow. Only when we accept all parts of our self can we grow beyond it and utilise it. In having awareness of self and then using all aspects of our self, they cannot and do not use us"

"Draw from and direct all aspects of oneself, do not allow different aspects of yourself to draw from and direct you"

"No matter if you're in a room, on a spacecraft in the middle of dark cold space, trapped between dimensions, underground, in prison, or on a beautiful sunny beach sun bathing. The Singular Truth within, the PRESENCE of your True Self remains with you, take this to the heart and remember it. For this power plus its great benevolence can be tapped into anywhere at any time with FOCUS"

"We only truly begin to live and find our self when we push off the shores of fear and into the great oceans of the loving unknown"

"Dive deep into your own soul, find the greatest most powerful parts of yourself and bring this treasure to the surface"

"Hold the vision and know it's yours"

"In order for something to have life and for the possibility to exist, One must live it now. Thus it LIVES and the manifestation can be brought forth into fruition"

"In order for something to exist, have form and live, it must be open to the possibility of its own existence"

"Everything has intelligence imbued into itself, cells, plants, water, even rock. All of creation knows its place and purpose"

"Water is a vibrant living essence that contains/holds memory and can be programmed"

"The atomic structure of water when focused upon realigns itself to the consciousness of the observer and reflects this state completely"

"Water is the lubricant between all dimensions and all omnipresent worlds"

"Water is the lubricant between all dimensions and all omnipresent worlds"

"Water is pure; it allows energy to flow without hindrance. The human body is mostly water to allow the electricity of the electric universe to flow"

"Crystal was the first form of complex life, they are alive and they hold specific vibrations and energies"

"Crystals can hold vast amounts of energy and information, be charged up with vast amounts of energy and information placed within its structure, or have all of this released"

"The universe is information. Crystal can store vast amounts of information in light imbued into its structure. Crystal is the most efficient, effective way to store information"

"We can do nothing alone. Friends and allies are important to have. Friends and allies sometimes help to aid, guide and counsel us during our journey of Oneness to the Singular Truth within. They help keep us anchored on the Golden Path, thus any missteps are lessened"

"Do not plant negative seeds that foment an environment of fear, chaos and confusion. Always plant positive seeds of awakening that sprout forth wisdom, peace and love"

"If you wish to live in a better world, one must become a better person, and then put in the work actively inside and outside. It is down to the individual to direct their own mind and their own destiny"

"The core of the occult is the predator energy that destroys worlds, vampires' energy and destroys life"

"God The Creator does not require worship, for God is perfect and already has everything it needs. If a/your God requires worship, it is obviously the wrong God"

"You are not useless, every small action and every small thing you do helps to alter the course of history for a better tomorrow. So be disciplined and consistent in applying yourself"

"Every creation, every item has its own energy and has a life of its own. You will feel magnetized to certain people, objects or items if they offer growth for your future, or they contain something you are missing or yet to explore and that you will need, they will resonate"

"Life is about learning and experiencing, by being and doing. You will magnetise events and beings that best suit your nature and that which your life is an example of, like attracts like. If you are negative the universe will provide you with lessons. If you are positive the universe will provide you with lessons."

"Do not say something unless it is worth speaking. Do not write something unless it is worth writing. Do not create something unless it is worth creating and it's truly needed"

"Everything contains within itself a deeper communication; allow the universe to speak to you. Capture its greatness, its mystery, its beauty, and its wonders, for all time"

"We are here but a short time within the scale of eternity. We are but a breathe, the snap of a firefly, the flap of wings, the flash within lightning, make the days count"

"The problems of an individual's life are small in comparison with the world as a whole"

"Giving in every act one can engage in is an art. Give where you can, when you can and how you can. But never over burden yourself, never knock yourself off centred balance or you will become destitute, poor and unable to carry on giving"

"Overtime refine your being and dissolve all your negative attributes or parts of oneself that do not serve you, whilst refining your being in all its positive attributes and becoming the loving living embodiment of them"

"The very wisest of beings should rise to positions of power within this world. Those who contain the most love not those who contain the most fear like today. The world is backwards"

"Just as you think the path is at its end a new path will be presented onto thee, a new door always opens for the path is infinite. The journey to True Self is infinite"

"Build communities within the worlds that encourage growth of the individual, based on love and truth. The Singular Truth within."

"Incorporate into your day, every single day the practice of inner listening, stillness is key to your total empowerment. In stillness all things can be known for in stillness your connected to all that is, was, and will ever be"

"A person has a certain capacity for things, such as love, peace, truth and wisdom. Pace yourself, be patient every day. For when you pass your capacity, the rewards for self are no longer rewards, they become destructive and all that was learned that day can be jeopardized"

"Allow the teachings to unlock new parts of yourself, unleash their energies, imbue this into your being to do their thing.

Do not rush"

"Expansive in thought, expansive in feeling, expansive in emotion. BE EXPANSIVE"

"Do not underestimate the power of discipline and consistency. Both will excel your life and your evolution forwards in quantum leaps"

"Train your will power daily, for there are those who are trained and those who are untrained. Being trained will give you a big advantage over all those who are not trained"

"All inherent skills and natural abilities inside an individual are neither good or evil. Like technology, it is how you use it that makes it so"

"A word, a song, a vision. A single spark can ignite the fires of awakening inside anyone"

"We come into the world alone, we leave the world alone. We meet people and beings who help us and aid us along our journey, but ultimately it is down to us"

"Everything starts and ends with you"

"Everything starts and ends with you"

"Once binded to someone on all levels, you are always binded to them on some level. Choose wisely"

"When holding love within, you have access to all information about all things, all of the time. Love is precious, always keep and hold your love within, for it makes you strong and powerful"

"Love is the pillar that holds the flood gates to EVERYWHERE, open"

"Become a sensitive instrument for the Singular Truth within, the more sensitive the better. For it offers full visionary insight and stability simultaneously"

"Meditate daily until you have a great deal of control over your emotions, thoughts, feelings, and actions. Direct them accordingly"

"Contribute your gifts, skills and abilities to humanity freely. Some people are dependent upon what you have, to spark the fire of their awakening. If you do not gift what you have others who are linked to you, even beyond your understanding or comprehension, may never awaken in this life at all"

"The more stillness you can hold within the more you will hear the symphony of the universe, the calling of the Angels and the trumpets of your destiny"

"If you are not fully unified within yourself, then you require healing. Thus everybody requires healing upon some level. Do not bury the parts of yourself that require healing, bring them to the surface and face them head on. Accept them, then transcend them"

"Transcend thy fear,

Transcend thy shadow.

Imbue and ascend with thy love"

"The best most suited optimal time to receive high wisdom is when all outside and inside chatter is quiet. For how can one focus in on one thing and hear within a sea of noise?"

"Everyday develop your skills of inner listening, for it is a powerful tool of your evolution"

"Your body is a receptacle for waveforms containing communications, keep it cleaned, keep it bathed, keep it pure"

"One cannot see if the mirror is foggy"

"Learn through all aspects of yourself, all ways possible, by all means necessary"

"How God the Creator built you was no accident, or the time or place you were born. Know thyself and unlock the secrets of who you are and your ingrained destiny"

"In stillness you know what you require, what you feel your missing, what you feel you need. Create it all; from that well spring of abundance within, plug the holes in the temple"

"Create clarity not confusion,

Create peace not war,

Create love not fear"

"When it comes to destiny, one must have unshakeable patience. You may be ready but they may not be. They may be ready but you may not be. Be Patient. Be Fearless"

"Allow things to unfold naturally, God created a perfect pace for things to work out for the best, always. Do not try to speed things up thinking you know better, for in this resistance it creates nothing but suffering for yourself and for all"

"To the highly sensitive and deeply insightful those who use the full power of the Singular Truth within, the outcome of relationships engaged in can be known from the outset"

"All realms and places you imagine exist, they exist somewhere in infinity. All places you dream, good and bad, exist simultaneously alongside your existence here. To the beings of other worlds, this world is the dream"

"You can't change in life that you were born different, but you can change your life so that you are different and make a difference"

"Names are not important you are not your name. It is but a label so you can operate in this world and dimension."

"All energy is curved, what we give we get back"

"Everything is a form of art and can be mastered to a high degree"

"There are two types of creator.
Conscious co-creator and unconscious"

"Wisdom can't be rushed neither its integration into your being or into your life, it requires the upmost patience, as does everything."

"There is no why, it just IS.

There is no try, just do or do not.

Take the path of certainty, never the middle ground, for this creates nothing but confusion and ultimately weakness"

"Anything is possible and most probable, when you bring down the barriers of doubt inside yourself"

"Treasure what you learn, for each thing when used and applied within the context of existence makes you very rich indeed"

"We are immersed within creation; we did not leave the higher dimensions to come here. We exist in both places simultaneously and are shrouded within the beautiful wondrous cloak of creation itself"

"You do not have a Soul, a Higher Self and a Deeper Greater Mind. You *are* these things"

"Everything you watch, see, feel and think becomes a part of who you are. Appreciate each experience and moment for enriching and adding to the divine wondrous splendour of Self that you are"

"Everything you see is unique.

Everything you feel is unique.

Everything you think is unique.

You are unique. Yet your uniqueness must be defined in terms of inclusion, not exclusion, to be truly at peace and free"

"It's our action that creates, makes and defines us. Always be doing something.

Never be apathetic"

"There never was and there is no such thing as a prophet. Do not live under the shadow of others or it will drain you, weaken you and ultimately destroy you. Learn for a time from others, but never shed your responsibility for being a messenger and a creator yourself"

"Everybody has a deeper communication to bring into the world, a cargo to deliver. Do not shed your own responsibility or lose yourself with any being who is proclaimed as a prophet, or you will fail to deliver you sacred unique gifts to the world."

"All disease is a form of disharmony within the creation, Harmony through vibration is also its cure"

"The more unified, harmonious and pure you are within, the more impervious to disease"

"Through us the world heals.

Through us greatness is allowed to flow.

Be open to giving and receiving, no ego.
Just allow your BEING-NESS"

"To have abundance within of all positive attributes such as stability, certainty of self, peace, love. Plus be impervious to chaos, confusion, disharmony and all negative influences. Connect deeply to, abide with, and embody the Singular Truth within"

"People are mirrors for Self, different people reflect back to you different aspects of yourself. Learn from this"

"Everything is one. This means all those beings who are not in balance with themselves, others and the creation/world, are unhealthy, have a disease and are mentally ill to a certain degree"

"As everything is one, when the world and people go out of balance to a certain degree and souls are disharmonious to the whole for too long. Be it nature itself or even higher powers, these forces will always step into to correct the imbalance. This is not judgment upon humanity, people or beings, but as all is one, it must be this way or the whole of creation would be destroyed over time"

"Balance must be kept. The oneness of all things must be implemented into daily life or there will always be dire consequences for humanity and all beings involved, eventually"

"There are enough resources on the world for all people to have abundance their whole lives, including those yet to be born, until the end of time. The problem is not overpopulation or lack of resources, it is mismanagement of those resources"

"You're a powerful creator; always create something to enrich your inner wealth. This will create internal stability and much peace, for being creative is our natural state"

"To create is to bring to life,

to bring to life is to love"

"To love is to be, to be is to exist"

"Always be creating possibilities in all things, be expansive in all things. Do not limit thy infinite potential with illusion of limited mind"

"Practice, practice, practice, practice. Meditate at least once daily, for this is the most powerful tool for empowerment of Self and reconnection to the Singular Truth within"

"During your daily mediations ask yourself is there anything you have missed, overlooked or that you need to know? This will allow all possibilities from the past and present to present themselves onto thee, so you can decide if you should pursue them or let them go"

"Accept reality as it is, not how you want it to be. Construct things from where you are right now, not from where you imagine them to be. This is the secret to true progress and real change in life"

"Surround yourself with people and beings as strong as or if not stronger than you are yourself. This will provide an environment of growth and stability for all"

"Align your focus, allow the Singular Truth within to flow naturally. Do not cultivate the darker angels; cultivate the better angels of one's soul."

"The biggest lies are to ourselves. There are many voices inside a person, follow the Golden Path/Thread of the heart for the truth is singular"

"Do not become possessed by the demons of your own fears. For stability and certainty of Self, in any moment you need. Always go within and commune with The Singular Truth in the deep ocean of your heart"

"Those who accept self-deception, will be destroyed and thus perish through that self-deception"

"Only take on what you can handle at any one time, no more or no less. Life is like a seesaw, Find the balance.
Give everything all of the time, every time. Go out of your way every time, all of the time. For Quantum Growth And Evolution of Spirit, The Singular Truth Within"

"Negative energies are destructive, grounding and constrictive in nature. Positive energies are Creative, Uplifting and Expansive in nature"

"Negative energies are unstable in there manifestation, positive energies are stable in there manifestation. Use Both Wisely ruled by the Heart, not the mind"

"Energy is constantly flowing like a river, flowing and pulsating through your being. Each emotion positive and negative is a lens to experience reality, direct the flow, direct your emotions, energies and awareness. Do not deny them or allow them to direct you"

"Only when negative energies direct you instead of you directing them do they destroy your soul"

"Separation from the creator and the Singular Truth within only leads to death and destruction, walk with the Creator always as closely as possible"

"Acknowledge your negative emotions; liberate your soul with the Singular Truth within"

"The powers of the negative and the positive are yours. The powers of Destruction or Creation. The powers of mind and of the heart. Connect with the Singular Living Truth within, thus it will grant you restraint, stability and allow you to use your powers wisely for the good of all life"

"The place that best suits that particular energy in space and time for it to complete its purpose, is always chosen as the place for it to manifest and have life"

"The Shetu and their allies have full control of the world economy; they can collapse it any day they do so choose. That is too much power over others for a group of beings to have. Total power over beings like this is called slavery. Do not allow this insanity to continue"

"With the Shetu and their allies controlling this world, Humanity is always upon the precipice of total disaster and even extinction itself. Be as self-sufficient as possible to ensure greater chance of survival"

"With the state of the world the way it is, always have at least three years supply of food and a good supply of water, able to filter endless/large supplies if required. This preparation is at the very least to be responsible"

"Preparation is most of the work; the actual doing is the smaller part. Both are equally important"

"Create new ways of

Seeing, Being, Thinking, PERCIEVING.

The world's symphony of destiny is in your hands"

"Know your value, know your worth.

Know yourself"

"Think of all things as seeds, whatever you plant you will sow. Through either seeds of fate binding or Destiny Enlightening"

"Be aware of your projections, use them as a tool. Learn the powers of projection both inside and outside. To be able to Project oneself on any level is a powerful ability"

"Project a PRESENCE of power, strength and certainty to avoid conflict"

"Be more scared of inaction and doing nothing, than taking action and doing something"

"Allow your work to serve you; do not allow your work to consume you"

"Use every weapon in your arsenal; use every spiritual bullet in your gun. Do not hold back, never stop. Apply yourself and the full totality of your being; apply your energies always, every day. Then freedoms victory and liberation of the Human race is an inevitable certainty"

"Every moment can birth a new life. A greater life. Always be open, always be ready."

"All energies such as truth and love are conscious living energies that get stronger over time if we embody them. Become binded in love, binded in truth. Thus binded with your destiny"

"When you make space in your life and within yourself, other energies are what thrusts your life forwards. You will witness these energies as people and events within reality"

"The first rule of love is to love yourself. The first rule of peace is to find it within yourself. The first rule of kindness is to find it within yourself. The first rule of happiness is to find it in yourself. You have everything you need within already, do not be a tyrant with yourself"

"Build capacity each day, have large capacity to allow greatness to flow through you and all other positive attributes, skills and abilities"

"While passing through the world, leave the best of yourself behind. Leave a legacy for future generations to create a world of love, compassion, truth, kindness, high wisdom and peace. Everything and anything that enriches the soul."

"Love your small victories, for one by one they add up to BIG ONES"

"SOL + U = SOUL"

"Create your ways; create your life in ways that work for you. Be original in all things, push the envelope. It is this PUSHING yourself to greater new heights that drives Humanity and the world forwards"

"All hierarchical structure is a distortion of oneness. All hierarchical structure is a bad thing, as all beings are equal. The structures of this world must be holographic in nature; they must be complete, whole, unified onto themselves. Where anybody good can rise to their full potential and the bad weeded out in the process of oneness"

"On your journey of truth upon the Golden Path, when you freely express yourself and being then hit resistance of a system, a factor that tries to limit your full potential or a control mechanism. This is like a map of the deception, this will clearly reveal and outline all the deception to you that most live under and are suppressed by.

Thus BE UNLIMITED, BE INFINITE and knock down ALL MAN MADE BARRIERS to reveal the truth.

Live a life based upon truth, not lies. Do not let any man or being limit the great mystery of your life and full wondrous power, beauty and splendour of your Inner Divine Self"

"Do not knock people down nor trample on the backs of others to get to where you are going. Although if they can accommodate the weight and they willingly want to help you and others, then it is ok. For all need help from time to time, no matter how strong they are. Native indigenous tribes know this well"

"If you are presented with an impossible task to accomplish, do not even spare a thought to think about it. JUST DO IT"

"Life never stops moving and always keeps coming, whatever you focus on spawns more of the same, over time"

"We are within an Ocean of Light, sound and motion. We are living within a hologram; build your structures in a holographic way"

"In order for you to have materially rich people, you have to have materially poor people. Thus not only have the materially rich placed themselves above poverty, they also create and maintain it"

"All the evil corrupt systems in this world are hierarchical in nature for it puts power in the hands of a few. Create a holographic structure for all to be equal and for all people to thrive in abundance"

"You are a Multidimensional Being of PRESENT LIGHT. Think that way"

"Do not try to gain advantaged in the short term in a temporal manner, at the expense of the future and big picture. Sacrifice the temporal comforts for the sake of the big picture and to bring it about"

"Always give yourself to something greater than yourself, to expand massively and advance yourself quickly. The energy is expansion"

"There is no such thing as a curse, it is fate manifested in your future through consequence of your action or inaction"

"Discern the Singular Truth inside each person as you navigate this world of life and in general. Become aware of where and when it's operating through a being or event, and when it is not"

"Look for the Singular Truth inside each person, disengage if it's not present. Engage if it's present. It is PRESENCE and the will of God The Creator operating deeply beneath the surface of things"

"Where the Singular Truth is PRESENT and where it is not are the only two things we can perceive within creation itself.

There is nothing outside of this"

"Navigate this world moment to moment with The Singular Truth within contained deep in your heart. Your Deeper Greater Intelligent Divine Mind and in true relationship with your Higher Self."

"If things in life are running smoothly, perfectly and in synch it means there is nothing blocking the energy flow. Thus the manifestation is complete onto itself and will express itself in a perfect manner. However if things start to go out of synch, mess up, deteriorate, it means the energy flow is blocked. Or there is energy attached to something that must be balanced and dealt with for it to proceed without hindrance to its full manifested glory"

"All dense negative energy forms pockets and sinks. The more light and positive energies rise upwards"

"All things are alive; when something has PRESENCE it has life."

"PRESENCE is LOVE. Always imbue PRESENCE into everything you create or want to manifest. PRESENCE keeps the manifestation ALIVE"

"Without PRESENCE the manifestations and creation itself deteriorates over time. Because in this universe the main constant is change"

"Always pump new energy and PRESENCE into your life so it does not stagnate and so the fractal holograph of your reality does not constrict through time, then eventually collapse and destroy itself"

"To live is to be PRESENT.

Stagnation is DEATH"

"Life is LOVE. For God The Creator gave up a part of itself, a part of its own body for you to be here and experience life. PRESENCE here comes with great responsibility, life is a scared gift, thus one must be PRESENT to expand, grow and thrive here"

"Preserve your energy at all costs, it is a scared gift and we only get a certain amount of it in life. Do not let any vampiric people or system draw it from you. Expand your energy capacity daily when and where you can through expansive endeavours"

"Cultivate yourself every day.

Cultivate expansion in everything you do, cultivate positive skills and attributes, cultivate virtues as habits. Cultivate each day all that is good"

"You have everything you need within already, all of the time. Offer to yourself that which you seek. To be part of the Wholehearted Living Tribe"

"Be aware of all your fixed patterns, or perception and behaviour. Do not allow these automatic parts of yourself to alienate you from your essence, or block you from being in relationship with your Higher Self. Dissolve them for all time in the Subtle Loving Infinite Ocean of The Singular Truth within"

"Do not complain about things, unless you are willing to resolve them. Complain Not, for the wise do not complain, they just resolve the situation. It wastes energy to complain"

"Sometimes one has to be lost within the world to find themselves. But if you are truly lost, always return to your original blueprint in life before anything happened and go from there"

"Always go with what you know, until something better comes along"

"If you meet an obstacle in life and it gets the better of you, simply apply more energy than you did before on the same area to defeat it"

"There is no such thing as failure; you only fail when you give up. Do not however waste your energy on fruitless endeavours"

"The Singular Truth within is highly discriminative, because it's time and energy has purpose and it has a job to do, a mission to complete. It cannot waste its sacred divine splendour on meaningless endeavour and pursuits"

"The very context of our existence is set within the creator, thus if we wish to be more peaceful, fulfilled and have stability within, our PRIMARY RELATIONSHIP must be with God the Creator. The Singular Truth within"

"Only draw from your past that which you can use in the present, do not ever allow your past to draw from you"

"There is no such thing as law of attraction. Align your focus to the reality you wish to magnetize; this is a responsible way to manifest so all will serve you. This is known as the Law of Shining. By becoming now that which you seek, you create it, without binding a shadow"

"When a new idea or concept comes into being and is manifested, it simultaneously manifests in many places at once and by many people. Because all is one and all minds are linked"

"When divine destiny presents itself, do not run away from the opportunities and hide in the shadows of your own mind"

"An intelligent being takes opportunities, a wise being creates them"

"Learn from nature, learn from everything around you. Stand tall firmly on your own two feet. Like a tree plant your roots deeply into the ground. Like a branch, be fluid and bend in the wind. Spread your seeds widely"

"Time = Suffering.

While upon the earth or within the cosmos.

Reduce, lower and dissolve suffering in any form for all, as much as possible. Alleviate it wherever and whenever possible"

"Energy needs to be balanced always. When negative energy is attached to a being and then cleared, it will always manifest as a negative event in one's life"

"When positive energy is gained, it will always manifest as a positive event in one's life. To balance the equation"

"Mankind always accepts the reality to which they are presented within. This is one of mankind's greatest strengths because of its adaptive ability and simultaneously its greatest weakness. For even a perpetual state of hell would be accepted as the way it is, unless a person knew differently or The Singular Truth within was strong"

"There is just God the Creator and you, all people/beings are equal, they have equal potential. Most suffer from giving power away to middlemen (The middleman syndrome). Do not give power away to middlemen; there is no need for them"

"Once a being is filled with new experience and the perception of itself and reality is expanded, its awareness never shrinks back to its original dimensions and it is impossible for it to do so"

"All beings are sensitive, to both light and dark. They either warm towards it or shrink away from it"

"God the Creator is great, anything is possible for God. It is amazing what God can do with a little water and sunlight"

"If you love flowers, let it BE, do not pick it. For possessing is not love or is it a need of the heart. It is a want of the Ego Mind, letting something BE as it was meant to be, is one of the greatest acts of love one can demonstrate"

"This universe is a great teacher. Nature is a teacher. Nature gives abundance freely. Observe its ancient wisdom and divine majesty, in the midst of the natural world's wondrous savage beauty, learn its lessons"

"Heaven and hell are both states of being. Both states can be easily observed in the human world and within the animal, insect and microbial kingdoms. All beings within this universe and the multiverse, live within the contrast of heaven and hell daily"

"Bathe in the stillness, the Light
And the LOVE"

"Be under no self-illusion or delusions,
give everything you have.
ALL OF THE TIME!"

"The power of stillness and its practical applications is unknown and underestimated by most. Meditate daily for the power lies in the stillness. Navigate the world through feeling, using the heart.

By listening carefully to all energy flow inside and out, a sensitive being can identify people, places and objects simply through feeling. For everything holds a specific unique energy"

"Stillness practice is the PRIME most important thing in spirituality. It's the thing that makes you sensitive so you can see deeper and be aware of more, it's the thing that makes you certain and stable, it's the thing that makes you POWERFUL, it is the thing that aligns you with God."

"God is still, everything else is in motion. You are a fragment of God the Creator, cloaked with creation"

"More information can be known in the silence and space in between, behind the scenes, than in what is actually said. To be aware of this truth of this is to gain the FULL COMMUNICATION"

"The infinite heart, the Singular Truth within, opens up the domain of feeling, let the heart open the full spectrum of reality to you and all its hidden depths.

The Infinite Heart is the gateway to Eden upon the Earth. For Eden exists right now and inside you right now, it just needs participation in the now to bring it about and anchor it here."

"The Singular Truth, is God inside the individual."

"What works for others may not work for you. What has worked in the past may not work for you anymore. We are constantly changing, listen deeply to the ebbs and flows, follow the will of your Deep Infinite Heart, The Singular Truth within."

"Fear of loss, fear of attachment, Fear of time going too fast. Fears.
Do not allow anything to slow or weight down your expressions of life."

"The journey of truth is a lifelong refining process that transforms you from one state of being and living, into another. It is not something that happens overnight, it requires daily work for your entire life."

"There was stable economy for hundreds of years, then bankers came and created instability.. All the instability and chaos in the world today is engineered fear.

TO THEM CHAOS PAYS"

"Natural Cycles have been Hijacked and Inverted to benefit the few. Consumerism is the engine of war. Fear keeps you apathetic and feeling powerless. But you are GREATER THAN THE WORLD"

"UNIFY WITHIN YOURSELF, JOIN FORCES WITH YOUR ALLIES. Your brothers, sisters and the indigenous and native tribes, we are all indigenous. Listen to them, they know what they speak about and they have bear witness to the atrocities, have been on the front lines, have faced it head on and still do today more than ever"

"Become present to yourself, for the living PRESENCE of God the Creator inside of you, is the ultimate protection against all forms of manifest evil, past, present and future"

"Respect your sacred temple, the body. You become a mix of all energies that you mix with and have ever mixed with forever altering your thinking, your mind, your DNA and consciousness for ever"

"Choose your partners wisely. For once mixed on all levels and connected upon those deepest levels, beings deal with all the baggage, residue and thought forms of one another good and bad"

"Love the NOW into the future"

"Seeking creates more seeking,

Being creates more BEING"

"Positive expansion in everything, then positive reinforcement"

"Any practice that promotes health, higher consciousness, and positive attributes is a good thing to take up"

"Certain facets of Human Beings can be understood, but the totality of the whole is beyond even the most wise"

"Yes it is important to have experiences, experiences so you are open to new ways of Living, Being and Thinking"

"Each generation thinks it's the first to invent and bear witness to life's experiences. But this is not the case, thus value The Wise Old Souls and Ancient Old Wisdom"

"The Two biggest killers within this world are money and LOVE in its many distorted forms. LOVE in its distorted forms is not love at all but something else entirely"

"One can create full pictures from fragments of the whole. Two can know the totality of the relationship from the outset, through its initial potential. All relationship can be known from the outset, THAT is the power of meditation and stillness"

"Meditate daily for at least 30 minutes; meditation creates certainty of self and stability. The POWER of God is STILL, for GOD IS STILL"

"Every day of life, every moment, always be expansive in all thought feeling and action. Then life only gets better, it's inevitable"

"Water is a great healer; it is a divine cleansing agent. Water cleanses away negativity, thought forms, surface dis-harmonics and residue"

"Master to a high degree the domains of the spiritual, emotional, mental and physical.
All levels of being"

"To be PRESENT is to be loving fully from the deepest part of your soul.
To be love is to be aware."

"It does not matter how much time you have spent with a person, it is the PRESENCE that is important."

"Bring more love into your life, bring more love into your world, bring more love into each moment. Love is the answer to everything."

"All stars and our sun are star gates that transform energy from one state to another, and allows energy and consciousness to pass from one dimension to another."

"Most people will do anything to disengage and escape reality, for PRESENCE comes with responsibility. BE PRESENT ALWAYS!"

"Be more PRESENT to yourself; be more PRESENT to your life. Everything is about PRESENCE"

"Be PRESENT to yourself internally and PRESENT to your own life externally"

"We are all evolving or devolving it depends how present we are to our own lives. Responsibility is the KEY"

"Different symbols, movies, songs, all structures, including memories all hold frequency, dimension and energy. Master this to a high degree and unleash these energies when you want and at will"

"Be expansive!

Always have an image of yourself to grow into, your best most powerful version"

"Do not be concerned or judge those who are doing no harm to others, be concerned and do something about those who are"

"Create anchor points within the world, a support system of people. So when you stumble or fall, like a trampoline, you can bounce quickly back to stability, normality and action"

"Always be mindful of your state, be constantly doing and thinking of ways to improve it in all areas and on all levels of being. BE ACTIVE!"

"Bring the full totality and presence of your being to every engagement."

"You cannot save the world, you cannot save another. Attempting to do so will destroy you and them, for each journey back to God the Creator is a personal one. However, one can heal the world and can heal peoples thinking. Be a healer"

"God the Creator does not force anything upon any level of being, love by its example. Let all things unfold naturally, all relationships and everything in relationship. Eventually your cup will run full, thus overflow into the world and onto everything"

"Mainstream media peddles illusion, delusion, fantasy, fairy tales and fake news. If you want real news, go to alternative media; go to people on the ground. Truth comes with responsibility, GET INVOLVED"

"Evolution Through action,
LOVEOLUTION"

"You are the LIVING TRUTH. TRUTH is not a pursuit or something you seek.
It is a way of LIFE AND BEING"

"Only take what you need, not what you want, keep the balance of the universe. The world is a mess because people want more; it is this very thing that robs them of themselves"

"To have true inner wealth one must create inner wealth, to have abundance one must give abundantly. Cultivate yourself daily and the better aspects of your nature"

"Anything that's created technologically that goes beyond creating self-sufficiency, becomes detrimental and is always used to enslave populations. So only take technology as far as becoming self- sufficient with what you have"

"Refine your being always higher, always outwardly, There's power in sacrificing things that are not necessary"

"The greatest hope within this world is not only the people themselves it's what we have already up to this point, and our creative flows of imagination from this point onward. Our duty is to anchor the ideas here and take action on it"

"First people need to work their own stuff out inside themselves and that will then create space, after a while, inside them where they can give to others. But not give to others and make themselves destitute or poor, in true relationship and balance"

"The languages of man are diverse nowadays in the modern world and people need to be able to identify the wolves from the sheep, or the pretenders from those who are real. If they can identify that, then that in itself will help them to stay clear of danger.

People and their labour will also be protected instead of being stolen from them"

"Do not carry around any baggage in your life outside, or within, or in any relationships that no longer serve you. Doing so not only holds you back, it holds them back to.

Be LIGHT, Be FREE to FLY"

"With each new question asked and then solved, with each new awareness gained, use it all. Realise the errors of your ways and make the appropriate changes moment to moment. This in itself shows great Strength, Courage and Wisdom"

"It is the spiritual realm where the true treasure and power lies, THAT inner realms wellbeing and integrity must be safeguarded at all costs inside the individual. The physical realm is easy to change, easier when one is focused and unified within"

"Detach the chords of chaos and confusion; attach the chords of Love and truth"

"Our lives are not our own. BE PRESENT to yourself and stand in your integrity always. For our lives are binded to others and if you do not stand within your power, other's lives will be drastically affected through time"

"Never destroy something good, if something works keep it going until you can no longer stand doing it. Then at its precipice transform it into something else entirely. Create, forge, and follow a new path but keep moving forwards, expanding, never stagnate yourself in life"

"The human being has perfection within but is imperfect itself. The human condition is about learning from mistakes and refining ones being to higher states. It is about gathering experience, expanding awareness but most importantly LIVING the full totality of the soul's perfect expression here right now"

"Heaven and hell, light and shadow.
Go hand in hand in this universe.
The secret is to accept people/beings as
they are and positively construct and
create from that point onwards. Not be
overtaken by the darker negative aspects
of one's inner nature and vampire beings
energies or destroy"

"Cultivate your skills of discernment and discretion every day. For the world is full of all extremes of good and bad mixed within beings/people"

"When fulfilling your greater work and destiny, things will reveal themselves naturally as you go. It is not a matter for the mind, but the heart"

"Anything that you receive in your deep heart, any words of wisdom that can be used to uplift the state of humanity to higher levels of consciousness and human experience. Write it down, save it, apply it and give it as a gift to humanity"

"Always stay active in all areas of your life to prevent decline in all your faculties, use it or lose it. Life is made to be lived, stay PRESENT"

"All art and words are like snapshots in time, showing a reflection of the being and the world at the time of their conception.

Value these freeze frames of time for their everlasting divine beauty, majesty and significance to heal the soul of Mankind for all time thereon after"

"If something works, keep it up and keep doing it, success is inevitable. If something does not work give it up, adapt and try something else. Always stay engaged with the Singular Truth within the heart, never be within the ego personal mind and take things personal. Will and perception is everything"

"If a butterfly was to flap its wings on one side of the world it could cause a tsunami or an earthquake on the other, this is known as the Butterfly Effect. Thus even the smallest of actions can have profound large effects upon the future"

"Without engagement of the heart, life is meaningless. People are merely hollow walking zombies, the walking dead, despite what image they project into the world or others. Being PRESENT to the world, being PRESENT to one another is the real gift. Being PRESENT with the full totality and every fibre of your being is what truly counts"

"Real EDEN is making a lasting positive difference on people's lives. So from that moment forwards they are a different being completely"

"If people were aware and able to recognise the subtle nature and the subtle influence of higher powers everybody would be very happy indeed. Be still and connect to the Singular Truth within, meditation daily is key. If you think you do not have time for meditation, meditate double that day without question!"

"Everything has intelligence within itself, from the microcosm to the macrocosm, from the inner realms to the external and outer realms"

"Do not just scratch the surface of life, dive deep. Life is about trying out and experiencing the full spectrum of extremes. Gathering experiences and enriching the soul"

"You will never exist the way you are right now; it will never come or exist again. Be PRESENT to yourself and live the sacred divine gift that life has to offer fully moment to moment"

"Fill your inner cave with beauty, warmth and wonder. With gems, diamonds, rubies, treasures of life's sacred eternal memory and experiences. For you do not want a barren, dark, cold cave when you leave this realm"

"In space the vast distance between inhabited worlds brings a great sense of Serenity, wonder and peace. As one glides between the stars, the great void is felt within the being and the vast scale of the unknown frontier is internalized like never before. One is at the forefront, the gateway of the great mystery to one's own existence and being. The Gateway to the future of all that is known, all that has been forgotten and all that is yet to come"

"Never give to charities within this world; most are set up purposely so the people you give to and want to help never receive the money or help you gave. They are in fact control mechanisms put in place to subdue the very people you want to help. The only way to be 100% sure of helping those who require it is to be DIRECTLY INVOLVED on the ground, get your own hands dirty, be PRESENT. You do not shed your own responsibility and it give to middle men. It is your responsibility to go and be there in person and see where the energy is used and applied across the entire journey"

"True Charity is being FULLY PRESENT"

"There are many ways to learn, it comes in many forms, we are always learning for the journey is never ending. Contrast of learning is good way to boosts ones evolution quickly"

"Let everything unfold naturally in the day and life, in so doing it leaves you very content, happy, peaceful, and fulfilled. Your cup then overflows into the world, the universe and people naturally, this is God the Creators way"

"Always be PRESENT!

That is the greatest lesson one can learn next to being love. Being PRESENT to oneself and others is the answer to everything in this Multiverse"

"Create space for it and it shall appear.

Build it and they shall come.

DO IT, DO IT, DO IT.

The appearance is birthed by the action,

Not the result"

"First you have to find the voice in your life that has never lied to you within life. The Singular Truth within. Then listen to only that voice and cultivate it daily, so it becomes louder, stronger and more powerful, it becomes the ONE unmistakable voice amongst all the voices speaking. People have millions of voices with them that are mostly false, go from that place of truth deep within. The Singular Truth"

"Look back through your life, all the decisions you made, through contrast recognize everything that went right and everything that went wrong. Identify the Singular Truth within, your one TRUE VOICE you can follow without question and with 100% certainty all of the time, anywhere"

"When you are deeply connected to the Greater Deeper Mind, the Singular Truth within and are in relationship with your true self/your Higher Self. You will naturally leave all that is unhealthy for you behind, people and relationships, beliefs, habits and habitual thinking, jobs, society and culture. All that kept you small and within a box will be dissolved and the Greatness that is within will then begin to FLOW through you and out into the world."

"Life never stops coming, it never ends, it is ever changing and PRESENT. Life in this world in its current state, will try to beat you down and steal your energy, your light. Do not allow this happen. Stand tall on your own two feet, bust down every barrier and obstacle with the full fury of your True Deep Heart, never hold back. We are growing, expanding and fighting for more than just ourselves"

"The more dispersed your energy the more weaker, confused and chaotic you become. The more Focused, Concentrated and PRESENT your energy the more powerful and strong you become. You really are a Multidimensional Being of PURE ENERGY"

"Mastering energy flows is like being a bowman or archer. You can hold the bow with its arrow ready to fire and let it go, but it goes nowhere and fails to reach its destination. But if one can pull back in a deep breathe, be patient and then allow the energy to build to its maximum potential before letting the bow and arrow go, it will fire forth quickly to its destination naturally and strike the target"

"True understanding comes after the experience of doing and never before, one cannot truly understand something until they have directly experienced it themselves"

"Self-Destructive tendencies to oneself, others and the world manifest from lack of self-love"

"To control energy, to guide it, hold it within until it reaches its climax and manipulate its flow, is an art"

"Focus upon yourself and others close to you, then once this is mastered to a high degree expand your circle naturally to encompass and embrace more and more, eventually all life"

"Nurture hopes, encourage ambitions, pick people up if they stumble. People stumble sometimes, so they can learn how to pick themselves up"

"We create everything good and bad by being PRESENT to ourselves, the world and others. This PRESENCE of being within people and beings can be used to identify the level of awareness of people and beings too. Be discerning and cultivate this skill daily and in all your engagements"

"The whole war game in this world being played out is so people give over freedom willingly for security.

The whole war on consciousness and people themselves is to convince people to give over their freedom willingly.

This war on consciousness and on the perceptions of the individual, is nothing less than the complete subjugation of the human race, it is the ultimate form of tyranny, a tyranny without bars where people imprison themselves.

But the good news is, it only works if people are disconnected from themselves and the Singular Truth within"

"This is a Free will Universe. Because people are conscious co-creators people are told ahead of time about events to steer their creational force in the favours of the architects of this reality. If you are not creating the present and future, somebody else is doing it for you. So be responsible and get engaged in conscious co-creation and the future you want to manifest and see"

"Preparation is one of the most important parts of any journey; the actual doing is the small part"

"Each day thank God the Creator for everything good in your life, we are very lucky. Now think of all those who have very little. This will keep you humbled and serve as a reminded to take action; we are within a world in need"

"Do not be a tyrant with your own mind. SELF-LOVE. It is a gift when your best friend is yourself. That is the best way! Self-love is the most important thing, only after this can you give to and love others"

"In a world being taken day by day and upon all levels it's not enough to just sit on the side-lines, be apathetic, do nothing and be a good person. Because there are people taking everything from you, others, even trying to take the future. For there is back hole within their hearts, an evil darkness and greed that will never be filled. You are placed within the world for a purpose and to do something"

"People enslave themselves, they create their own chains and bind themselves to the capacity level they have for truth, at that time"

"Unslave yourself; expand your capacity for truth, peace, freedom and all things that are good, every single day"

"My only sadness and sorrow comes from the fact that we are here for a very short amount of time and that I will not get to personally know every member of the human family one by one. But over time in our many forms and incarnations, we will. That put a big smile on my face, for God is the total sum of ALL RELATIONSHIP"

"In the past there have always been distractions within the world. But today there is more distraction in the world than ever before, more music, more movies, more stimulation in ever expanding new forms and in ever expanding archives year on year. To cultivate your FOCUS as an ability and FOCUS now on what is truly important in life is more important than ever before"

"Thirst to explore the full spectrum of human experience while here"

"Those who seek power over others have already lost the war. They can slow the flow of information and can slow down the communication process, but cannot stop the flow of information. The truth always comes to light, breaks the surface and is far more powerful than they will ever be"

"Do not take any actions in life

Where fear is your motivator"

"The original intent and thoughts of something is of prime importance. This primal chord is what first strikes the heart of another and imparts the essence of the deeper communication. Allowing people and beings to understand it, as originally conceived and from any point in time and space"

"A person has many facets, be mindful of which one you are engaging with. Engaging with The Singular Truth within a person or not engaging with it are the only two things one can possibly perceive in the universe. Thus all one must do is, be mindful of where it is operating in the individual or engagement, and where it is not."

"Be mindful where The Singular Truth is operating within other beings and individuals and where it is not. Engage when it is PRESENT, disengage and save your energy when it is not"

"After engaging with other people and having social events always have time out afterwards to reflect on things. For different people, objects and environments draw out of you different things and there is much valuable information that will be revealed on reflection and through introspection."

"Life is a GREAT TEACHER, listen well"

"Everything is communication. On intense or important subjects or topics communication is best done face to face to lessen distortion"

"When it comes to creating things in accordance with God the Creators GREATER PLAN and to stay as fit, healthy and in balance as possible. The less mind the better, the more mind the more distortion. This applies to ALL THINGS"

"People are passing through life like ships on an ocean at night, one must navigate the ocean of life in what best way suits them as they go, but bring no harm to themselves or others. For one does not need to bring others down, stand upon them or destroy others to get to where you are going. Everything you need is already within yourself"

"It is good to every once in a while have a clear out inside and out. Release the dense old energies and anchor in the new high energies"

"A healthy, loving, caring and nurturing environment over time will heal all ills within a Human and any being and upon all levels. This is an inevitability, for Love truly does conquer all"

"God the Creator has already won the war, but Gods children continue to fight. You cannot wage war upon LOVE"

"Everybody gives a part of themselves to you either good or bad. People have contributed a little something of themselves to make you the person you are today. You are the total sum of all your integrated relationships and experiences"

"There are two forms of listening, listening externally and listening within, internally. Master both to a high degree to gain full advantage of all communication"

"There is more information communicated within the spaces, stillness and pauses, than within the form and movement itself"

"Sacrificing the unnecessary and meaningless for the meaningful and necessary is no sacrifice at all"

"Do not make any decision based upon fear. Face all your small fears and larger fears head on, all of the time! For they offer massive amounts of growth in equal reflection to the amount of fear felt"

"Everything evil and bad that happens within this world, is either planned or binded by fate"

"Protect LIFE and life force at all costs, life spawns life"

"Do not allow yourself to be disconnected from what is truly important, from the things that are vital and necessary. Mother Earth, the jungles, the seas, the deserts and the icescapes, the rhythm and heartbeat of LIFE itself"

"Experiences are necessary to help you have the right tools equipped to survive life and to evolve"

"All beings have many layers of being-ness to get through to get to the core of who they truly are, however the heart pierces them all simultaneously"

"Always speak and take action from the heart, because of the heart and for the heart"

"The face of God can never be seen or known. For it is beyond comprehension, it is beyond form and dimension, it is beyond light. GOD created these tools as a medium of exchange, thus the ultimate experience for being-ness to have of God, may only be felt"

"Everything is based upon energy, learn to conserve and preserve it. Direct its flow with full focus and its full totality whenever necessary"

"Life upon earth and life in the universe goes through a natural cycle of abundance, destruction, and rebirth. Humanity is deep within this cycle and our race is living within the ruins of what we once were"

"Upon the earth, from the higher states of consciousness to the lower, it's a world of extremes where the full spectrum is played out. The language is diverse too, also playing out the full spectrum of good and evil. Be discerning, discernment is a necessary skill to be cultivated daily"

"In a world of hell, of fear, chaos, darkness, of instability and uncertainty, good always prevails. So fear not, you have already won. For it is your WORK and your VISION, your ACTION, and the very act of you're DOING to bring it about that makes you victorious"

"When people unite under one will they become stronger than the sum of all of their individual parts. Unite with all the other parts of yourself through space and time. For all misery and suffering within Humanity itself is caused by one simple misconception. That we are separate"

"All suffering within the Human family and universe is caused by perceived separation from each other, from the world and universe and most importantly from God the Creator. But there is none.

ALL IS ONE"

"Anything that you think has power over you is merely teaching you how to stand upon your own two feet, remind you of your power, BE the power you already have within and express its full totality within the world fearlessly"

"You will never raise Eden by playing by the rules; these are the self-proclaimed slave masters rules. They do not live by them anyway. Break all the rules, The Singular Truth Within will guide your action and always abide with you moment to moment"

"Bringing something pure like Eden or your true self into a unpure environment/world will not be a cosy ride. It will take you beyond where you have ever been before, stretch you to the very limits of who you are and upon all levels completely almost destroy you, changing your state of consciousness and being forever more. But then within this natural birthing process of empowerment of Self, in this state of transcendence and Pure Focal Stillness, it will Put you back together stronger and more unified and more powerful than ever before"

"We are not made to be alone for long periods, we are made to connect, expand, collect experience and grow"

"Align with the Singular Truth within, all abilities and skills amplify profoundly. Then do your work in the world to magnetize others to you naturally. This flow of bringing remarkable beings together naturally creates the power to allow them to become something more as a whole"

"All governments are corrupt from their inception. Governments need a poor sub class to maintain power. The word government means mind control and they are a direct reflection of the power vacuum and responsibility given up with inside the individual, reflecting on the outside as a manifest structure. Simply give no power away any longer, they need you we do not need them, never have or ever will"

"Government likes to makes you dependent upon them for their own safety and security, for their own survival, not yours"

"Money is energy. The humans and beings who have architected this world/society will try to get you to spend your money on worthless dross; they will vampire your energies and life force and give you nothing in return"

"Create an environment of High Light within yourself and outside, the dark cannot survive within this environment. Then stand your ground in-dominantly inside and out, for all of your existence here and for all time"

"Dark cannot survive in an environment of High Light. Like a light make it bright, make it VERY BRIGHT within this domain"

"Every being has a weakness. You must recognize yours, pour lots of energy into this specific area and turn them into strengths"

"Any true relationship between two people is based upon giving to one another. Thus one simple question must be asked from the outset if you're truly ready for one. Are you ready to give everything to another, everything they need? To fulfil everything they dream of and do so desire?"

"Everything in this universe contains a teaching; nothing ceases to be, good or bad, until the lesson of it is learned"

"Being spiritual and unified within to a high degree does not prevent evil and darkness in your life; it teaches you how to grow strong within the shade and shadows of it until you dissolve it"

"Follow the golden path laid before your feet by the Singular Truth within. Establish a relationship with your Higher Self, be true to yourself always. Do not care what culture, society, the world or others think. Forge your own path as an example for all mankind and life"

"God gave you a part of itself; you are a soul, a divine spark. This is the Singular Truth that dwells within you. Thus walk closely with this part of God inside yourself moment to moment, because the closer you are to God the creator of all things, the stronger, more powerful and certain you are in everything you do"

"Fear is birthed within an individual's consciousness, the moment something the being loves is taken away"

"Only speak if it is worth saying, only write if it is worth writing, only take action if it is worth doing"

"When it comes to trust of another being, let your heart and its voice the Singular Truth Within be your guide, if a being has taken certain actions in life, know that

At the very least they are capable of doing the very same thing again, if not more. Thus know a being through all of their combined action up to that point in time,

Not their words"

"You do not need to go to dangerous extremes of experience to feel alive, for this shows lack of understanding and of self-love, it can also be self-destructive And can destroy you completely. It is PRESENCE of your being within any moment that determines how fulfilled and ALIVE you feel"

"Being PRESENT fully in the moment and accepting the responsibility that goes along with this is all that separates the entire spectrum of the Human race from one another. It is this level of PRESENCE you need to be aware of in other being's, to measure their state of mind and being from moment to moment"

"How PRESENT are you to other people and beings? How PRESENT are they to you? Being aware of this can help you conserve your vital energy and save you much pain and suffering if it is misplaced"

"How PRESENT are you to all the different aspects of yourself in life?
Physical, emotional, creational, mental, spiritual? Balance them all daily; neglect no part of yourself to be the most powerful expression and version of yourself within the world"

"It is said every person has a price and
also something they place value upon"

"Concentrate your energy; focus only upon what is truly important, necessary, meaningful and vital"

"Look into every aspect of your life and everything within your life. Ask yourself does it have integrity? If not, make minor adjustments, change it and cultivate a new space for growth"

"BE LIGHT like a feather in the wind, nothing should be held as belief, but only as a MEANS or TOOL to understand"

"POUR ENERGY into all your weaknesses every day, give them extra work and watch them transform into strengths"

"Do not go to others you do not know and who have not earned your trust, while within a weakened state. Do not give power away"

"If you understand either the context or the dimension of where you are, then the means to navigate it will be so much easier"

"The human reality could not exist in the state we are within without the reptilian world before ours. That is why we have a reptilian brain and animalistic beast qualities. This world and dimension is built upon the realities and level of consciousness that came before now. Just like the next phase of evolution for us and our race as a whole cannot exist without the human part of the story"

"Every thought, every action, what's then followed through moves the Human race either a little closer to the light or further away from it over time. Thus be mindful always of your manifestations and actions, plus those beings you choose to ally with"

"Time is your greatest asset; do not give time away without great purpose"

"You get binded to fate through actions within your life or inaction on what you should already be doing. To free yourself follow your true north, follow your destiny wholeheartedly and do not hold back"

"Experience is a powerful force of Transcendence, be proud. For no one can take away your experience"

"Everybody has a gift they must give. A gift given to them and imbued into their being by God the Creator before you we're born and with a great purpose. You must dedicate your life find out what it is, cultivate and develop it through life and gift it to humanity and the world freely"

"Those in a position of power within the world and universe will never educate or teach you knowledge of how to supplant them"

"Freedom is not having many choices and being able to do as you wish. Freedom is knowing you only have one choice, the Golden Path of the Singular Truth within that will lead you to the greatest expression and version of yourself while your within this world/universe, and fulfil Your Destiny wholeheartedly"

"The Singular Truth is the living truth within you, the voice of God itself, the part of you that never left God, your guide, conscience and council"

"There is no such thing as a teacher, for all people and beings outside only guide you into your own power. Thus align with Your INNER TEACHER. The Singular living truth within the deep core of your heart"

"The end is but a new beginning,

The journey always starts at the end"

Daniel is a property renovator/investor and lives in a small cottage in the Lincolnshire Wolds, in the UK, an area of outstanding natural beauty.

He enjoys nature, the countryside, and the natural rhythm of earth, life, and the Universe itself. He loves stillness and practices this each day and upon each hour.

Each day he takes time out to go into Deeper Relationship with his Higher Self and allows his Greater Deeper mind to emerge, becoming a more powerful embodiment of it day by day. Within this Deep Sacred State of meditation, and sometimes spontaneously throughout the day or night, the Deeper Currents and Pearls of Wisdom that are received from the deeper sacred space within are written down as Gifts for all.

Wisdom of the Eternal was birthed forth from this deeper communication with God the Creator. It is a Revelation for All Times and All People. Use the Insights and Knowledge, apply it in your life and in the world well, for it was meant for you and Now you have received it.

"BE L((((O))))VE"

You can contact Daniel through

his **email** for business enquiries

danielofdoriaa@gmail.com

or visit his

You Tube channel for more information.

https://www.youtube.com/user/danielofdoriaa

Made in the USA
Columbia, SC
14 June 2019